WORD by WORD

PRIMARY

LEVEL B PHONICS WORKBOOK

Steven J. Molinsky • Bill Bliss

Illustrated by
Richard E. Hill

Longman

Picture Dictionary / Level B Workbook Correlation

This correlation indicates how the activity pages in this workbook coordinate with the lessons in the *Word by Word Primary Phonics Picture Dictionary*.

Picture Dictionary pages	Level B Workbook pages	Picture Dictionary pages	Level B Workbook pages	Picture Dictionary pages	Level B Workbook pages
2–3	1–2	51	105–106	127	165
4–5	3–4	52–55	107–108	128	166
6	5	56–57	109	129	167–168
8	6–8	58–59	110	130–131	169–170
9	9–11	60–62	111	132–133	171–173
10	12–14	64	112–113	134–135	174
11	15–17	65	114–115	136–137	175
12	18–20	66	116–117	138–139	176–177
13	21–23	67	118–120	140–141	178
14	24–28	68	121	142–144	179–180
15	29–31	69	122	146–147	181–182
16	32–34	70	123	148	183
17	35–37	71	124	149	184
18	38–40	72	125	150	185
19	41–43	73	126–127	151	186
20	44–46	74	128	152–153	187
21	47–51	75	129	154–155	188
22	52–53	76–77	130–131	156–157	189–190
23	54–55	78–79	132	158–159	191–192
24	56–57	80	133	160–161	193–194
25	58–59	81	134	162–163	195
26	60–63	82	135	164–165	196–197
27	64–65	83	136	166–167	198–199
28	66–67	84	137	168	200
29	68–69	85	138	169	201
30	70–71	86–87	139–140	170	202–203
31	72–73	88–89	141–142	171	204
32	74–75	90	143	172	205–207
33	76–77	91	144	173	208
34	78–79	92–95	145	174	209
35	80–81	96–97	146	175	210
36	82–84	98–99	147	176	211
37	85	100–101	148	177	212
38	86	102–103	149	178	213
39	87–88	104–105	150	180–181	214–215
40	89	106–108	151	182–183	216–217
41	90–91	110–111	152	184–185	218–219
42	92	112–113	153	186–187	220–221
43	93–94	114–115	154	188	222
44	95	116–117	155–156	189	223
45	96–97	118–119	157–158	190–191	224
46	98	120–121	159	192–193	225
47	99–100	122–123	160–161	194	226
48	101	124	162	195	227
49	102–103	125	163	196–197	228
50	104	126	164	198–199	229

Pearson Education, 10 Bank St.,
White Plains, NY 10606

ISBN 0-13-022167-8

Printed in the United States of America

10   9   8   7   6   5   4

CONTENTS

Note: The symbol ← in this workbook indicates a word in the past tense.

Editorial Director: *Allen Ascher*
Executive Editor: *Anne Stribling*
Director of Design and Production: *Rhea Banker*
Associate Director of Electronic Publishing: *Aliza Greenblatt*
Production Manager: *Ray Keating*
Senior Manufacturing Manager: *Patrice Fraccio*

Manufacturing Buyer: *Edith Pullman*
Digital Layout Specialists, Page Compositors, Interior Designers: *Rachel Baumann-Weber, Paula Williams, Wendy Wolf*
Associate Art Director: *Ann France*
Cover Artists: *Richard E. Hill, Carey Davies*
Illustrations: *Richard E. Hill*

M	V	N	A	(M)
E	F	B	E	H
B	R	B	P	E
A	Y	X	A	V
C	O	Q	G	C

i	(i)	t	l	k
n	u	h	m	n
c	e	o	c	a
b	h	b	d	k
q	p	d	b	q

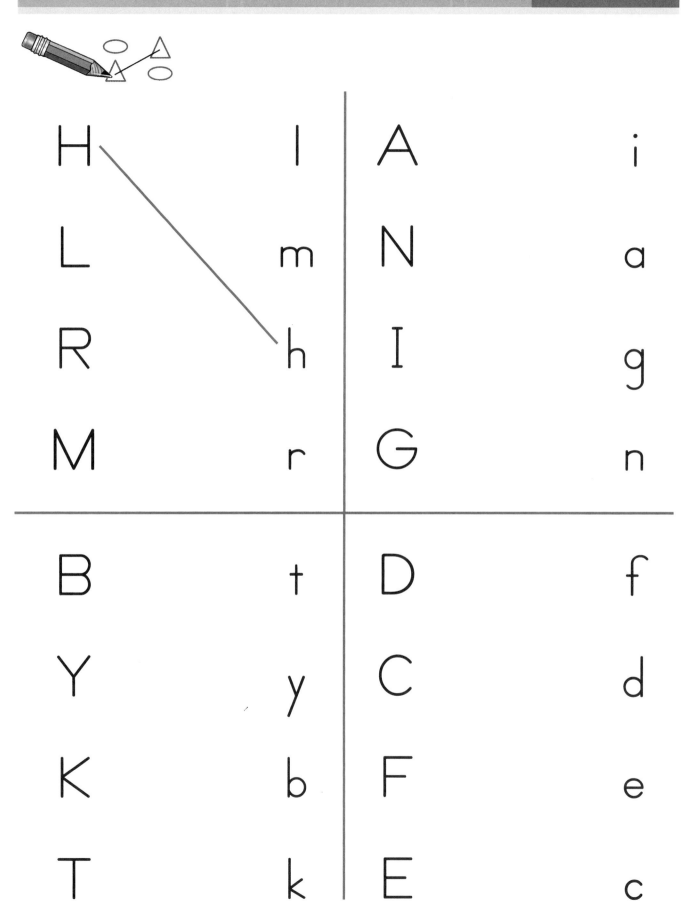

H	I	A	i
L	m	N	a
R	h	I	g
M	r	G	n
B	t	D	f
Y	y	C	d
K	b	F	e
T	k	E	c

D	H	B	(D)	P
V	U	W	Y	V
O	Q	O	D	C
R	R	B	P	F
G	Q	C	D	G

i	(i)	j	h	l
u	n	u	v	w
g	y	j	p	g
d	h	b	d	q
p	q	d	b	p

R	g	H	y
G	j	D	h
J	t	M	d
T	r	Y	m

F	G	†	g
R	F	r	t
G	V	g	a
V	R	a	r

m   (v)

m   v

van   (man)

van   man

m v

van van

an

an

van	man	man	van	van	man
a man in a van		a man in a van			

c   c   p

    can

   pan   can

c   p   v

pan   pan

an

an

an

| can | pan | can | van | man | pan |

a man and a can and a pan in a van

 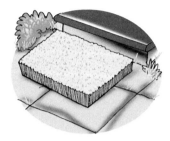 

m (b) c   m b c   m b c

bat   can   (cat)

mat   bat   cat

can   man   mat

b   c   m

cat   cat

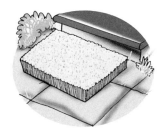

at

at

at

cat   can   bat   pan   man   mat

a man and a cat and a bat in a van

m (c) l   m c l   m c l

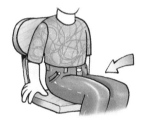

map   lap   cap

lap   can   cap

map   man   lap

L l

M m

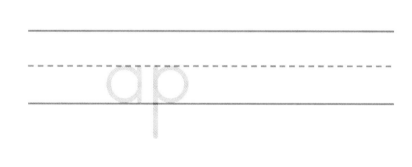

cap	can	map	man	van	lap

a map and a cap and a mat in a van

17

b p (w)   b p w   b p w

lap   bat   (big)

wig   map   pig

big   pig   pan

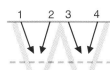

w b p

pig   pig

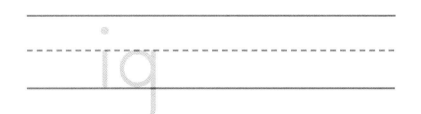

ig

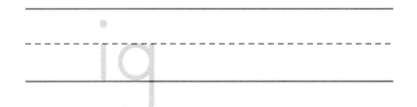

ig

ig

pig	pan	big	bat	wig	map

a pig and a cat in a big van

(k) p s   k p s   k p s

pit   (sit)   kit

cat   pit   kit

pit   pan   sit

Kk

Ss

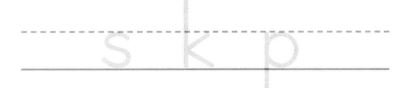

sit   sit

it

it

it

pit   pig   kit   big   sit   wig

Sit on a big pig in a wig.

d (r) z   d r z   d r z

   sit   rip   (zip)

   kit   dip   rip

   zip   wig   rip

Z z

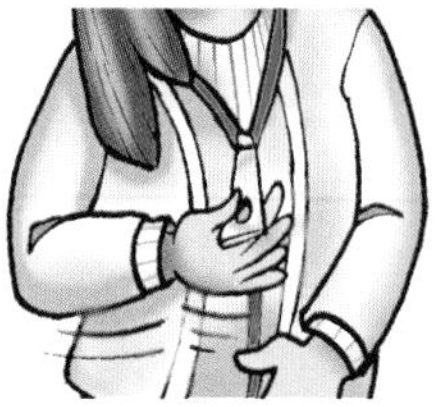

Z

z

zip

ZIP

rip

1.

2.

3.

4.

5.

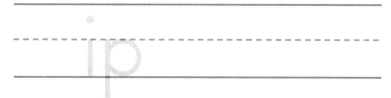

| rip | pit | dip | big | zip | sit |

A pig and a cat rip a cap.

28

(w) f p   w f p   w f p

pit   (pin)   fin

fin   wig   win

fin   pin   kit

29

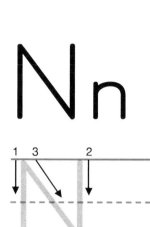

1 3   2

N

1
    2

F f

1 2

3

1

2

w f p

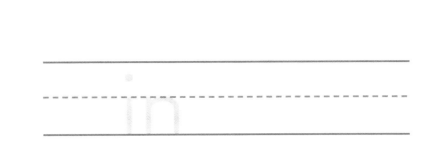

fin   fin

in

in

in

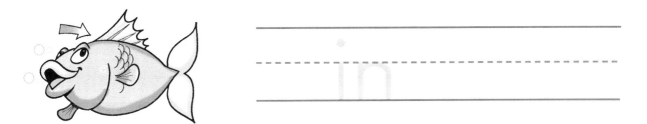

pin   pit   pig   win   wig   fin

Win a wig and a big pin with a fin.

l （f） h   l f h   l f h

   log   (hog)   fog

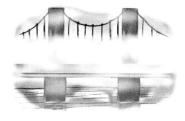   fog   log   hog

   hog   lap   log

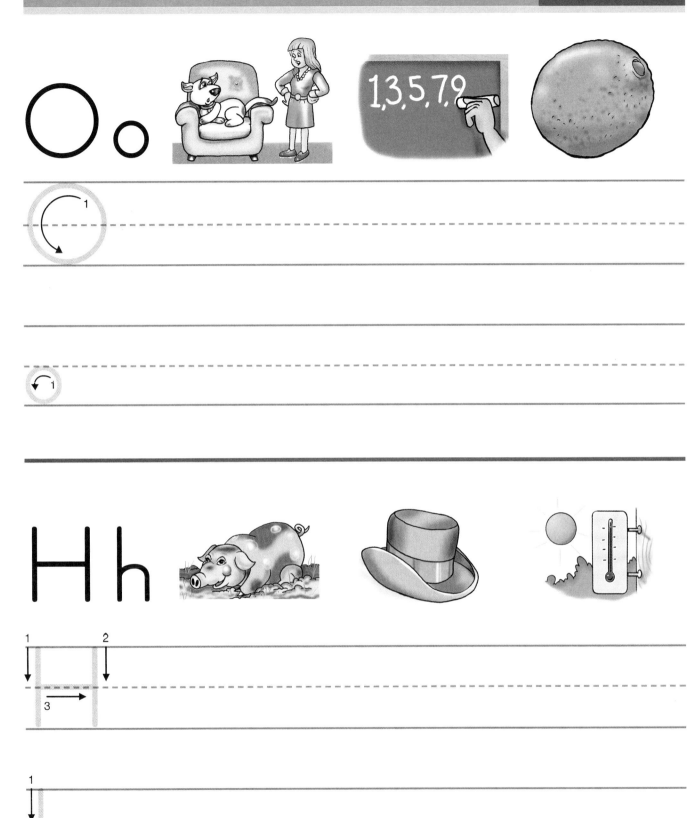

l f h

hog hog

og

og

og

log	hog	fog	fin	lap	log

Sit with a hog on a log in the fog.

  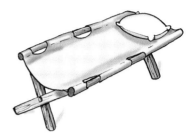

c h (p)   c h p   c h p

   (hot)   cot   hog

   cat   pot   cot

   pit   pot   hot

T t

1 →
2 ↓ T

1
2 → t

pit

mat

cot

c h p

hot   hot

ot

ot

ot

| hot | hat | pit | pot | cat | cot |

A hog and a cat sit on a cot.

m h (t)   m h t   m h t

   men   ten   (hen)

- -

   hen   men   map

- -

   men   hot   ten

men

hen

ten

h m t

men   men

en

en

en

hen   hot   ten   map   men   man

A hen and a pig sit on a mat.

n   p   (g)   n   p   g   n   p   g

get   pet   (net)

pit   pot   pet

hot   get   pet

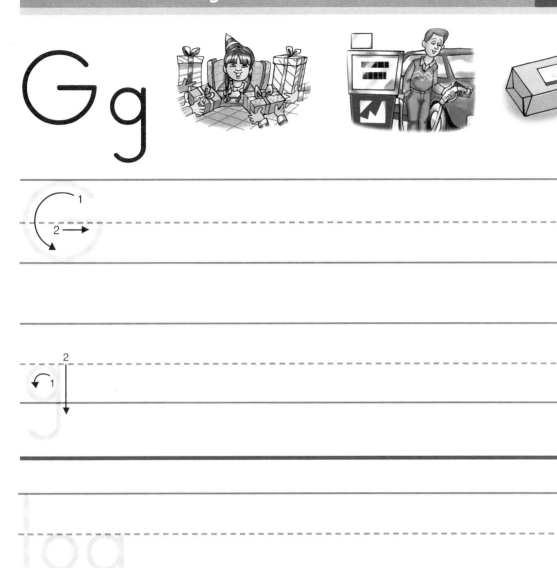

log

big

pig

n p g

net   net

et

et

et

pet	pit	get	pot	net	ten

Ten men get a big net.

r (s) b   r s b   r s b

(run)   sun   bun

bat   big   bun

sit   sun   run

sun

bat

rip

r   s   b

run   run

un

un

un

bun   bat   run   rip   sit   sun

A hen and a hog sit in the hot sun.

(m) b j   m b j   m b j

   big   [bug]   jug

- -

   run   mat   mug

- -

   get   jug   bug

Jj

j

j

jug

bun

map

48

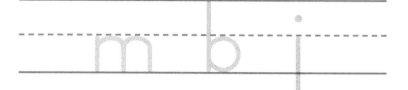

m b j

bug bug

ug

ug

ug

bug bun mug jug big bug

A jug and a pot sit in the hot sun.

1.

2.

3.

4.

5.

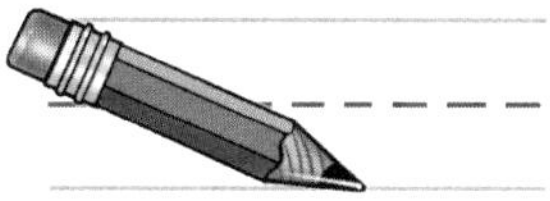

1. pig ✔

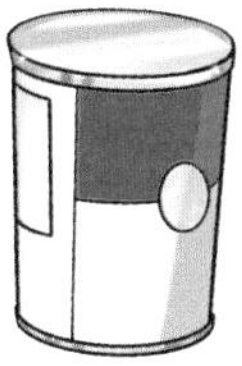

2. ca

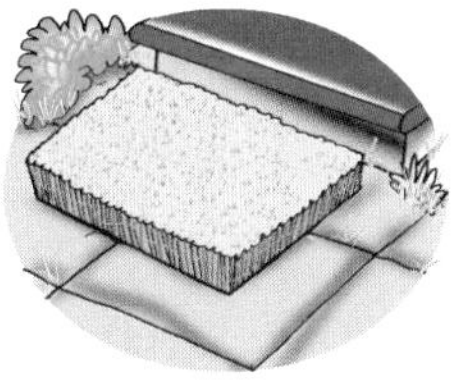

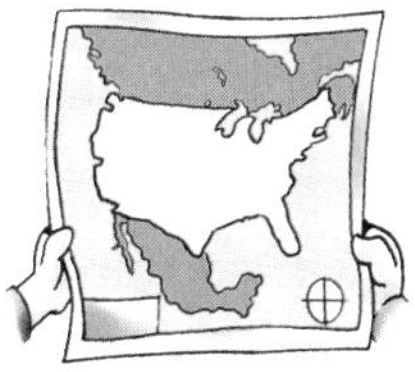

3. ma

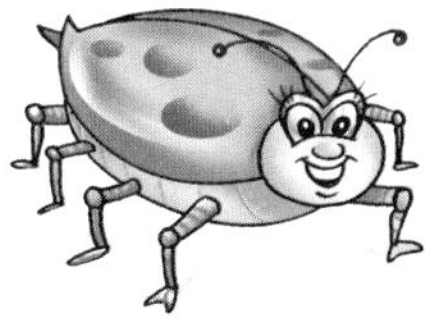

4. bu

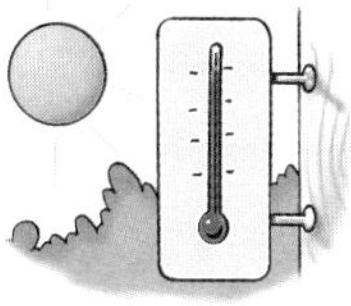

5. ho

m (f) p   c r v   c t m   f p r

   fan   pan   (man)   tan

   van   ran   can   man

   ten   fan   pan   tan

   fin   fan   tan   man

fan

pan

pan

man

ran

can

van

tan

can

ran

van

| fan | fin | run | ran | ten | tan |

Dan and Jan ran in the hot sun.

53

n   s   (m)   n   g   c   c   t   l   s   l   r

   sap   gap   lap   (cap)

   log   lap   tap   rap

   map   nap   gap   tap

   sap   cap   nap   rap

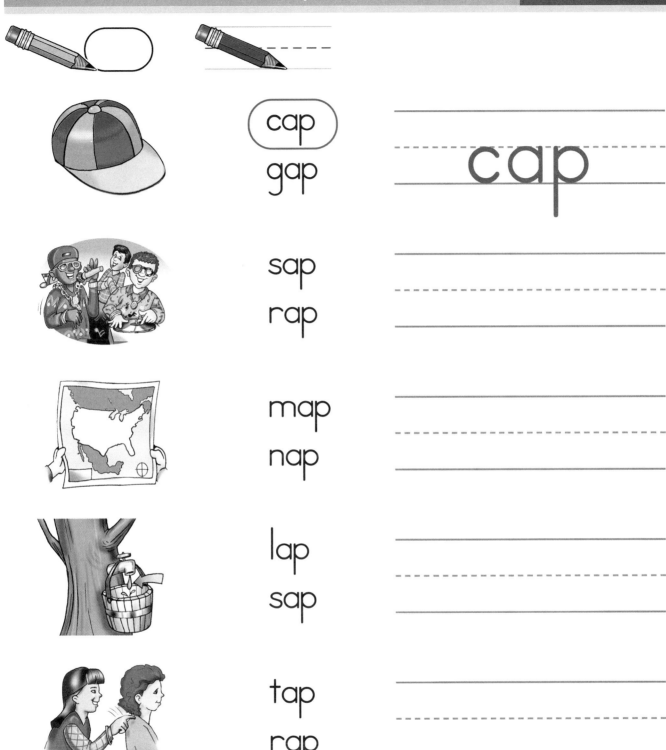

cap
gap

cap

sap
rap

map
nap

lap
sap

tap
rap

| rap | ran | cap | can | pan | nap |

Get a cap and get a map.

s (c) v   m n f   v b r   h v f

rat   fat   (bat)   mat

vat   hat   sat   cat

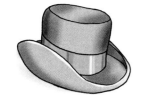

fat   sat   cat   mat

cat   mat   rat   sat

hat
(bat)

bat

cat
sat

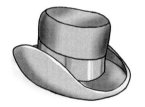

fat
hat

fat
vat

rat
mat

| cat | cap | can | map | man | mat |

A cat and a rat sat on a big mat.

p   s   (b)   l   d   p   p   s   l   m   b   s

 **(pad)**   dad   sad   bad

 bad   sad   lad   mad

 sad   mad   pad   lad

 bad   mad   pad   sad

pad
dad

pad

mad
sad

lad
mad

bad
pad

lad
dad

mad	mat	sad	sap	lap	lad

A sad lad sat on a lap.

 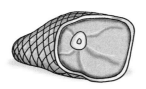

h (w) r   b t j   r y h   y j t

bag (tag) ham yam

jam wag dam rag

rag ham wag dam

yam jam ham rag

DICTIONARY
page 26

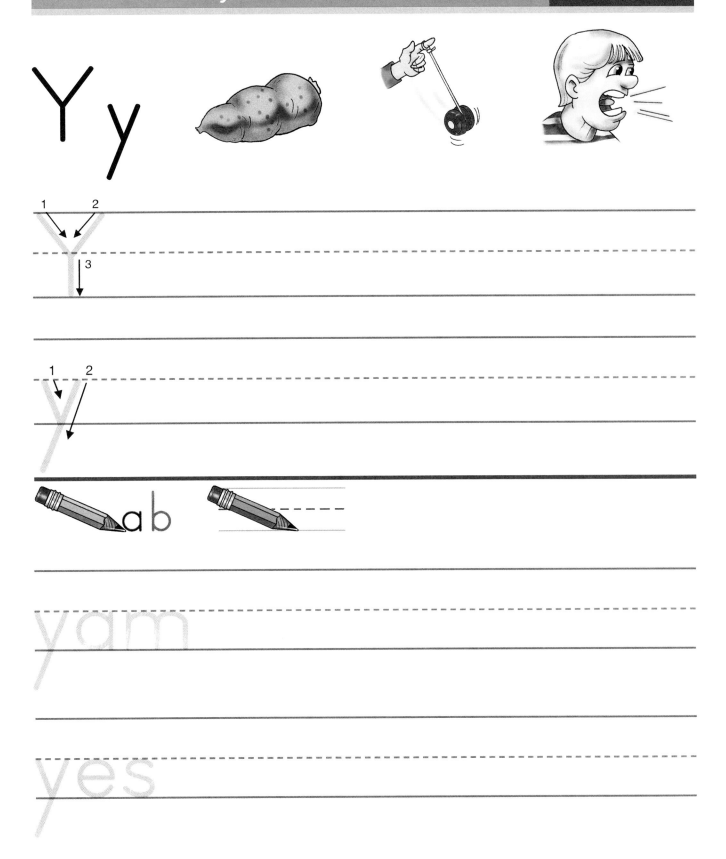

yam

yes

1. _____ ✔ bag

2. _____ _____ ag

3. _____ _____ ag

4. _____ _____ am

5. _____ _____ am

rag
(wag)

wag

tag
rag

jam
yam

jam
ham

bag
dam

bag   bad   bat   tag   tap   jam

Get jam, ham, and a yam in a big bag.

(p) f b   b j d   b d f   r p j

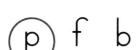

 fig pig (big) dig

 wig rig jig pig

 big dig jig rig

 wig fig big jig

fig
(wig)

wig

dig
fig

big
rig

pig
dig

jig
rig

big bag rag rig wig wag

A pig and a big cat dig and dig.

r (l) z   r   t   h   z   d   s   r   t   h

 (rip)   tip   lip   hip

 sip   dip   zip   rip

 hip   dip   lip   tip

 hip   sip   dip   tip

(lip) zip

rip sip

tip zip

dip rip

hip dip

tip

dip   dig   rip   rig   tag   tip

Rip a rag and dip it in a big vat.

SHORT VOWEL WORD FAMILY *it*

f   b   (p)   k   s   z   l   h   b   f   k   h

sit   pit   (fit)   lit

kit   bit   hit   pit

zit   bit   sit   lit

fit   sit   hit   zit

zit
(sit)

sit

kit
lit

pit
lit

hit
fit

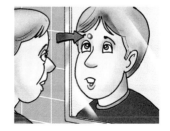

bit
zit

bit	bat	hit	hot	sit	sat

A bat hit a cat and bit a rat.

  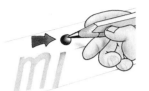 

g (h) l   p t d   c g d   l p g

 (cot)   tot   pot   hot

get   dot   tot   got

dot   pot   tot   hot

hog   hot   lot   cot

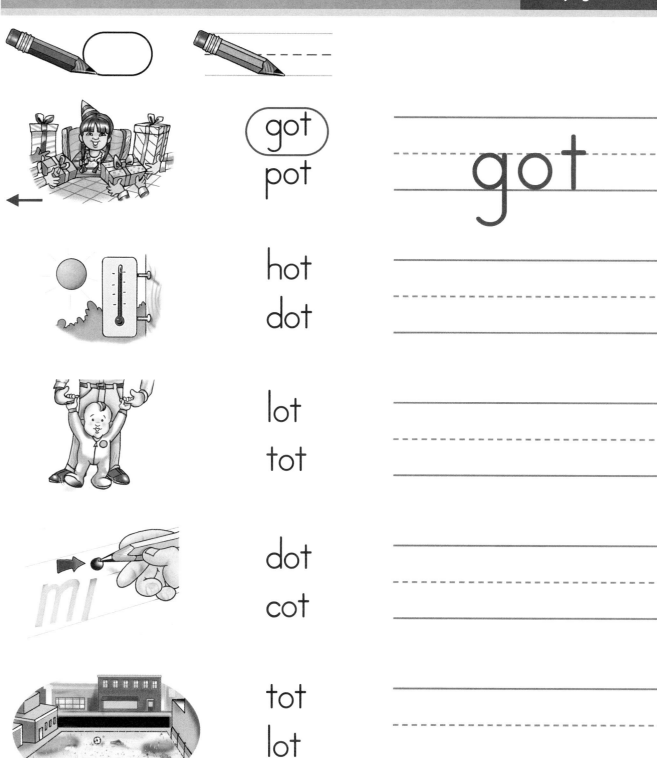

(got)
pot

got

hot
dot

lot
tot

dot
cot

tot
lot

| got | get | hot | hat | pot | pit |

A tot sat on a big cot.

b h (f)   m l t   h p m   h f b

fog   log   (bog)   top

hog   hop   mop   log

tap   tip   pot   top

mop   pop   top   hop

bog
(fog)

fog

log
pop

hop
top

mop
hog

top
bog

| bog | bag | big | tip | tap | top |

Hop on a log in a big bog.

 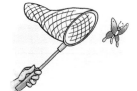  

j (g) p   n s m   v w j   p w v

   pit   pot   jet   (pet)

   jet   get   pet   met

   sit   sat   set   net

   net   met   pet   vet

74

pet
get

pet

jet
get

set
jet

net
met

vet
wet

set   sat   get   got   pot   pet

The vet and the pet met on a jet.

(h) t d   m p h   m t d   p h t

ten   (pen)   Ben   men

men   ten   hen   den

den   Ken   hen   pen

men   pen   Len   ten

den
(pen)

pen

ten
den

men
hen

den
ten

man
men

pin   pen   pan   tan   ten   men

A hen sat in a big den.

t (d) j   b t h   m j t   d r b

   dug   tug   (jug)   rug

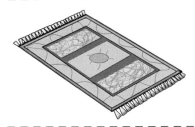   rug   bug   hug   dug

   mug   tug   bug   hug

   hug   bug   tug   dug

(rug)
mug

rug

tug
hug

dug
bug

tug
jug

dug
jug

| bug | bag | big | rag | rug | tug |

A wet bug sat in a big jug.

(r) f b   c h s   s c n   h n r

   (fun)   sun   rut   hut

   run   nut   rut   bun

   fun   hut   cut   nut

   cut   sun   hut   rut

sun
(run)

run

fun
bun

nut
hut

sun
cut

run
rut

fun	fan	hut	hit	cut	cot

Get a hot bun and cut it.

s   c   (t)   r   s   c   c   p   b   m   r   b

   tub   sub   (rub)   cub

- -

   cup   cub   pup   bud

- -

   sub   cup   bud   pup

- -

   mud   bud   rub   tub

tub
bud

tub

sub
cup

rub
bud

cub
cup

rub
pup

| cub | cup | cap | bad | bud | bug |

The cub and the pup sit in the mud.

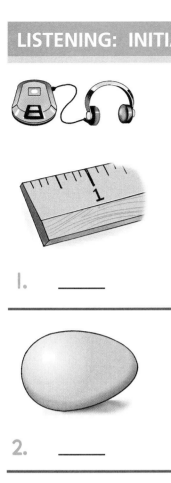

1.  _____  ✔ ill

2. _____ _____ gg

3. _____ _____ dd

4.  _____  _____  p

5.  _____  _____ 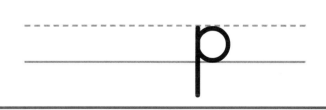 n

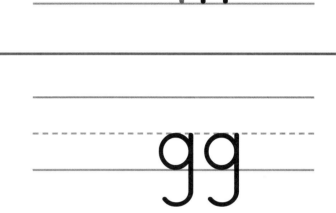

a e i o u

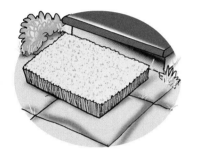  

m a t   m _ t   m _ d

m _ t   m _ ll   m _ p

mat   man   men   mop   mug   mill

Mud is on the mop and the mat.

a e i o u

n e t   n _ t   n _ p

n _ d   _ n _ t   n _ t

| not | nut | nit | net | Nat | nap |

The nit is not on the neck.

1.

mud

2.

3.

4.

5.

a e i o u

f i n

f o g

f n

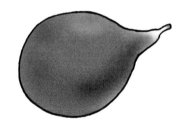

f d

f g

f n

| fan | fun | fin | fog | fig | fed |

Nat fed the fat pig a big fig.

 a b

a e i o u

 s a t s _ n s _ p

s _ b s _ t s _ d

| sit | set | sat | sob | sub | sun |

Sit in the sub. Sit in the sun.

LISTENING: CONSONANTS *f*, *s* + SHORT VOWELS

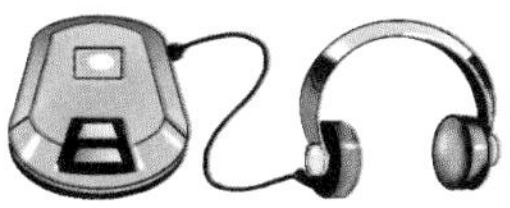

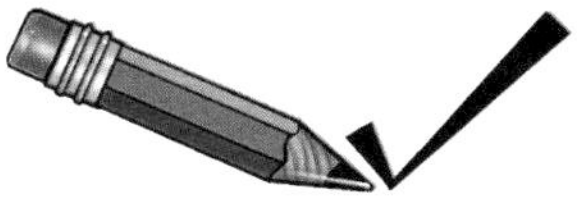

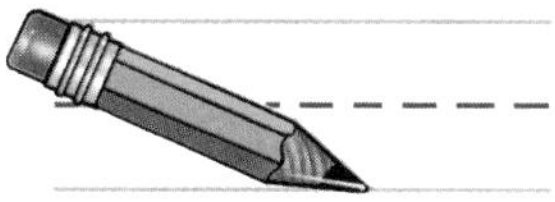

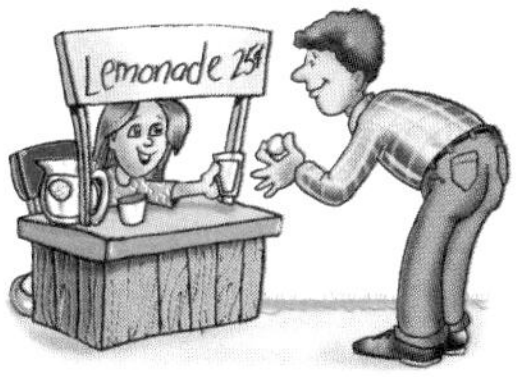

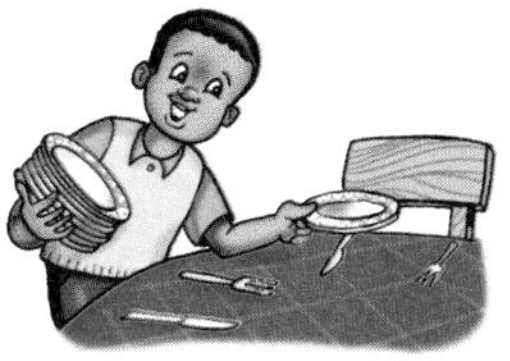

1. ____ ✔ set

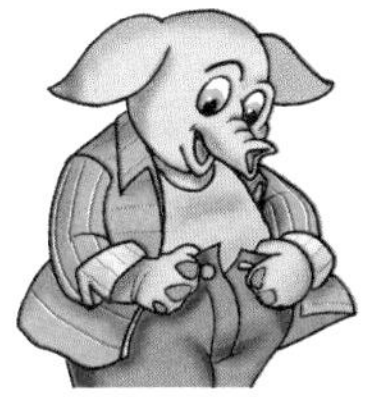

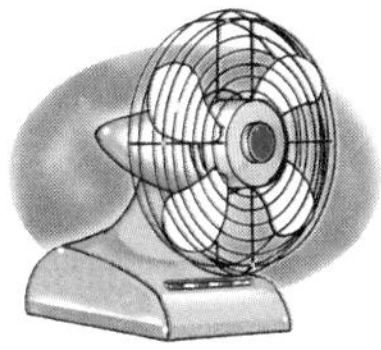

2. ____ ____

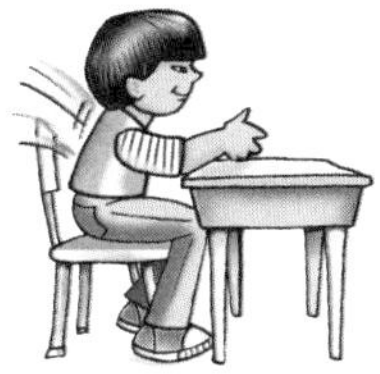

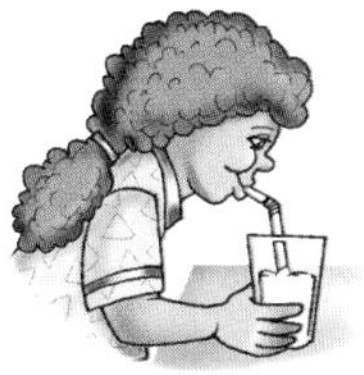

3. ____ ____

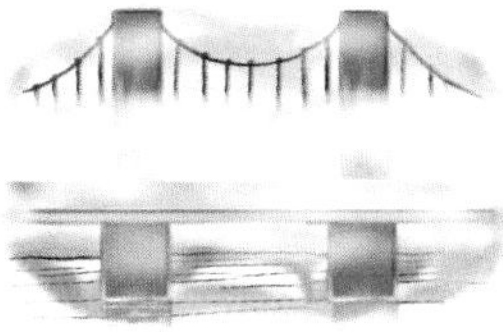

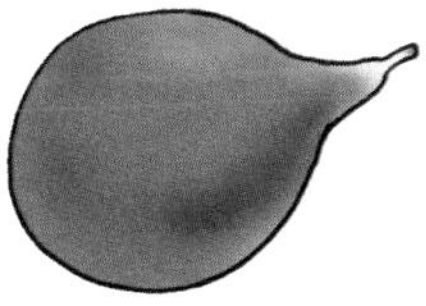

4. ____ ____

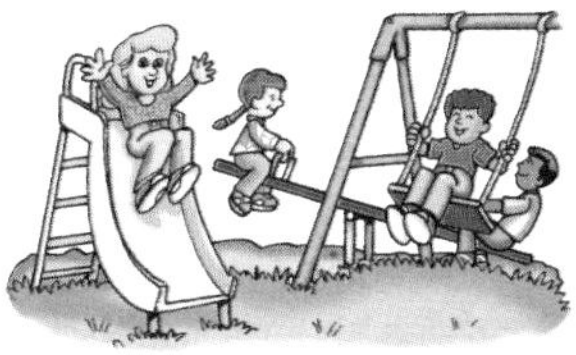

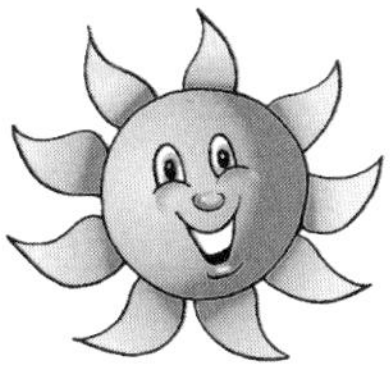

5. ____ ____

 a b

a e i o u

h e m   h t   h g

h m   h n   h p

hut	hit	hat	hip	hop	hen

The hog and the hen hop in the hut.

a e i o u

j u g   j _ t   j _ m

j _ b   j _ g   j _ g

jig   jug   jog   Jack   jam   jet

Jeff and Jill sell jam to Jack.

1. ✔ _____   _____   hit

2. _____   _____

3. _____   _____

4. _____   _____

5. _____   _____

a e i o u

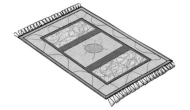  

rug r t r p

r d r d r n

rat   ran   rig   rug   red   rod

The red rod is on the rock.

 ab

a e i o u

l o g l p l g

l p l d l t

lot	log	leg	led	lad	lap

The lad led us to the lot.

1. log

 a b

a e i o u

b a g   b s   b d

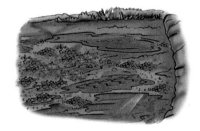

b b   b g   b t

| bug | bag | big | beg | bog | bus |

Bob is on the bus with a big bag.

 a b

a e i o u

p e n   p _ d   p _ p

p _ _   p _ n   p _ t

| pen | pan | pin | pup | pop | pet |

The pup sat with a pad and a pen.

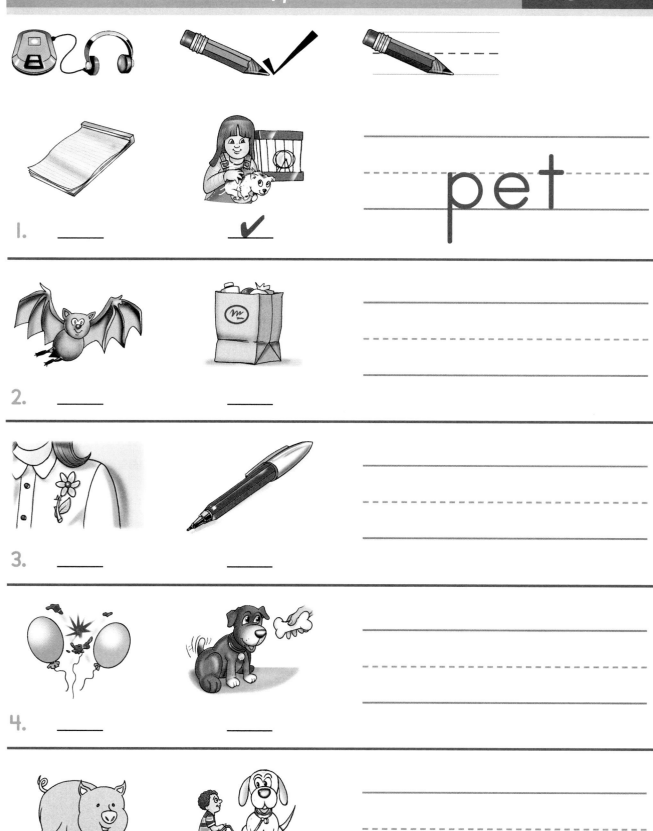

1. ____

✔

pet

2. ____ ____

3. ____ ____

4. ____ ____

5. ____ ____

a e i o u

d i g   d __ m   d __ n

 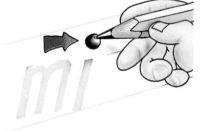 

d __ p   d __ t   d __ ck

| dig | dip | dot | dad | duck | den |

Dad is in the den with the duck.

a e i o u

t u b

t a g

t p

t n

t p

t g

tip	top	ten	tan	tag	tug

Tell the tot the top is in the tub.

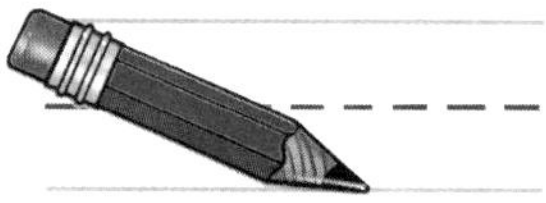

1. _____   ✔   tag

2. _____   _____

3. _____   _____

4. _____   _____

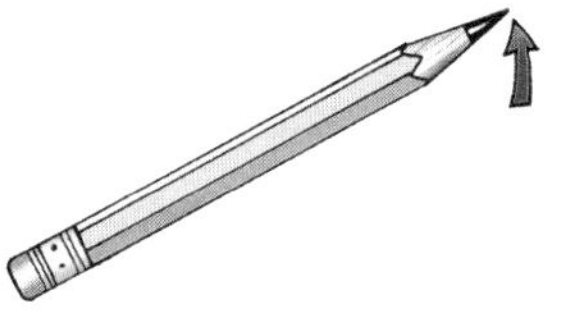

5. _____   _____

a e i o u

 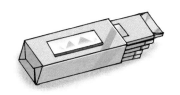 

g e t   g   m   g   s

g   ll   g   t   g   p

get	got	gas	gull	gill	gap

Bob got gum and Jill got gas.

a b _____

_a_ _e_ _i_ _o_ _u_

c u t   k _ d   c _ d

c _ t   c _ b   c _ t

cat   cut   kit   cot   can   Ken

Get the kit!   The cat got a cut!

105

1.

    get

2.

3.

4.

5.

   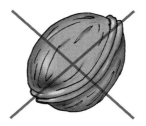

107

(t)
p

t
(p)

t
(p)

(t)
p

---

t
n

t
n

t
n

t
n

---

s
b

s
b

s
b

s
b

---

p
n

p
n

p
n

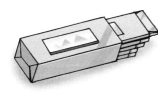

p
n

---

m
g

m
g

m
g

m
g

---

t
p

t
p

t
p

t
p

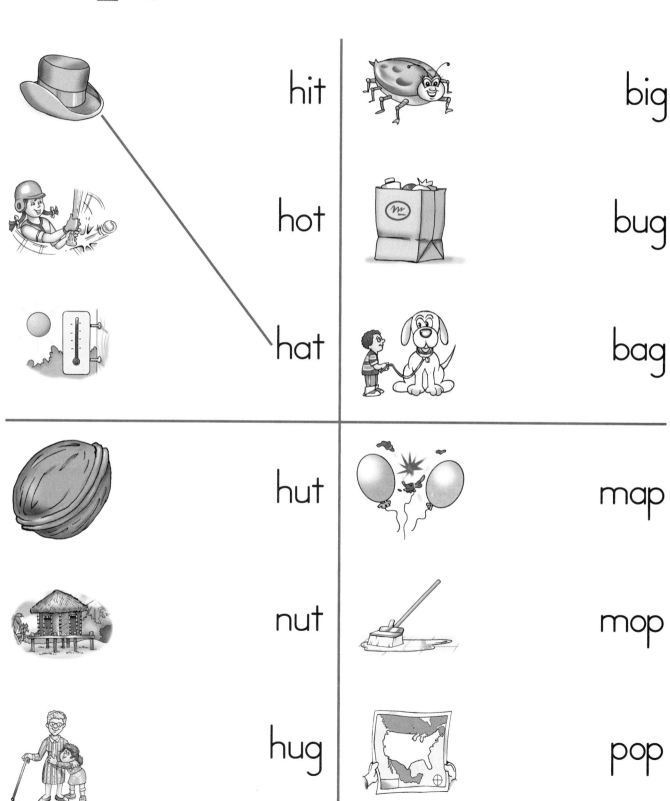

hit

hot

hat

big

bug

bag

hut

nut

hug

map

mop

pop

INITIAL CONSONANT BLENDS *cl, fl*

cl (fl)   cl fl   cl fl   cl fl

   flag   clap   (club)   flip

   flap   clip   clap   clam

   lip   flip   lap   flap

   flip   lap   lip   flap

 a b

cl fl

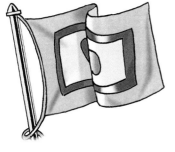

fl ag

ub

ip

ip

ap

at

| lip | clip | lap | clap | cub | club |

The flag is flat.   The cub can clap.

113

(dr) tr   tr fr   dr cr   dr fr

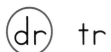

   crop   (crab)   trap   frog

   fan   ran   frog   Fran

   trap   tot   trot   drop

   trap   flag   drum   crop

 ab

cr dr fr tr

dr um

og

ab

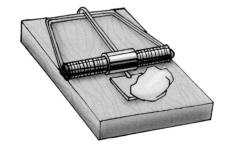

ap

op

op

| tap | rap | trap | fan | ran | Fran |

The crab and the frog drop the drum.

| sk (sl) | sm sk | sl sk | sm sl |

 slip   smog   sell   (smell)

 slip   sip   skip   skin

 led   sled   slug   skip

 sip   lip   skip   slip

sk   sl   sm

s l ed   ip   og

ug   ell   in

sip	lip	slip	skip	lot	slot

Skip in the lot. Slip on the sled.

sp (st)   st sw   st sp   sw st

   (stick)   stem   step   stop

- -

   stop   spot   pin   spin

- -

   step   top   stop   spot

- -

   stop   top   spot   pot

sp   st   sw

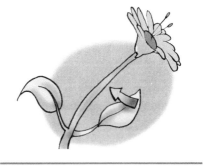

st em

in

im

ap

ep

ot

pin	spin	pot	spot	top	stop

Spin the top.   Step on the stick.

1. _____ _____✔

2. _____ _____

3. _____ _____

4. _____ _____

5. _____ _____

6. _____ _____

7. _____ _____

8. _____ _____

9. _____ _____

10. _____ _____

ramp
(lamp)

lamp

jump
bump

stamp
camp

dump
bump

hump
jump

| cap | camp | lap | lamp | ramp | rap |

Jump on the ramp. Jump on the bump.

(hand)
sand

hand

mend
wind

pond
stand

band
bend

band
bend

| win | wind | sad | sand | bad | band |

The band can stand in the sand.

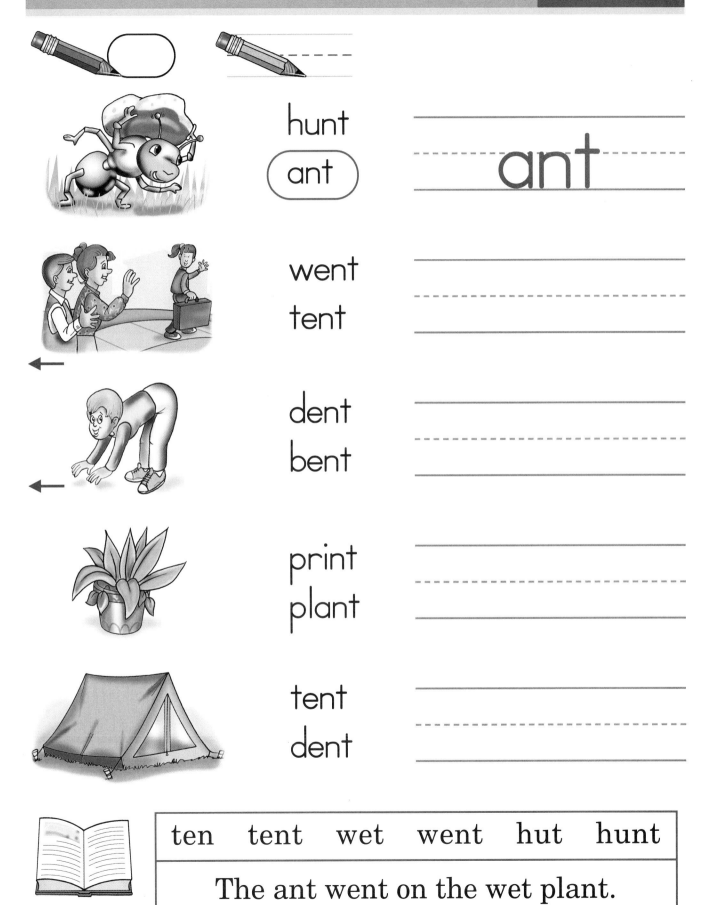

hunt
ant

ant

went
tent

dent
bent

print
plant

tent
dent

ten   tent   wet   went   hut   hunt

The ant went on the wet plant.

lk lt ft

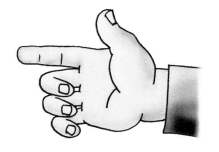  

left   mi____   be____

e____   me____   gi____

| rat | raft | met | melt | lit | lift |

Lift the gift. The milk is on the left.

(fast)
vest

fast

rest
nest

test
west

last
best

vest
rest

net   nest   fat   fast   west   wet

Run fast, run best, and rest.

 ab

st   sk

ma**sk**

de

li

du

a   sk

cru

| lit   list   last   fit   fist   fast |
| Dust the desk. Dust the disk. |

126

1.  _____    ✔

2.  _____    _____

3.  _____    _____

4.  _____    _____

5.  _____    _____

6.  _____    _____

7.  _____    _____

8.  _____    _____

9.  _____    _____

10.  _____   _____

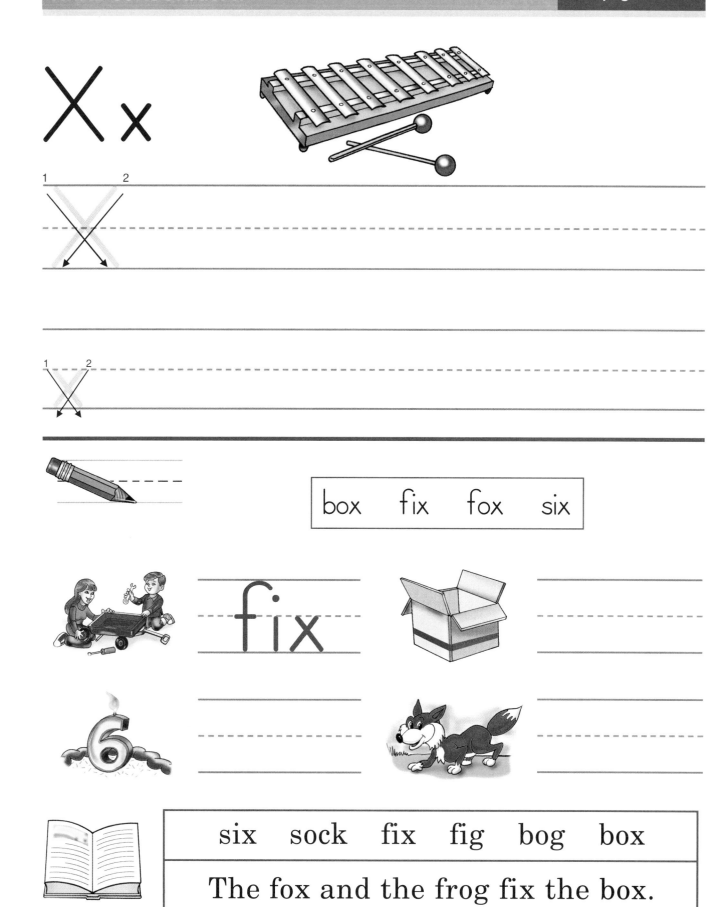

box   fix   fox   six

fix

six   sock   fix   fig   bog   box

The fox and the frog fix the box.

ss   ff

  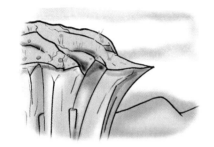

glass   dre___   cli___

ki___   hu___   cla___

| class | glass | grass | kiss | fix | cliff |

The dress is in the box in the class.

DICTIONARY
pages 76–77

ill
hill

sell
fell

shell
smell

gull
gill

c a t

spill
spell

fill   fell   spill   spell   sell   shell

The bell fell in the well on the hill.

| Bill | Fill | Spell | Spill | Tell | Yell |

Fill the glass.

_____ Jill.

_____ at the gull.

_____ is ill.

_____ the milk.

_____ cat.

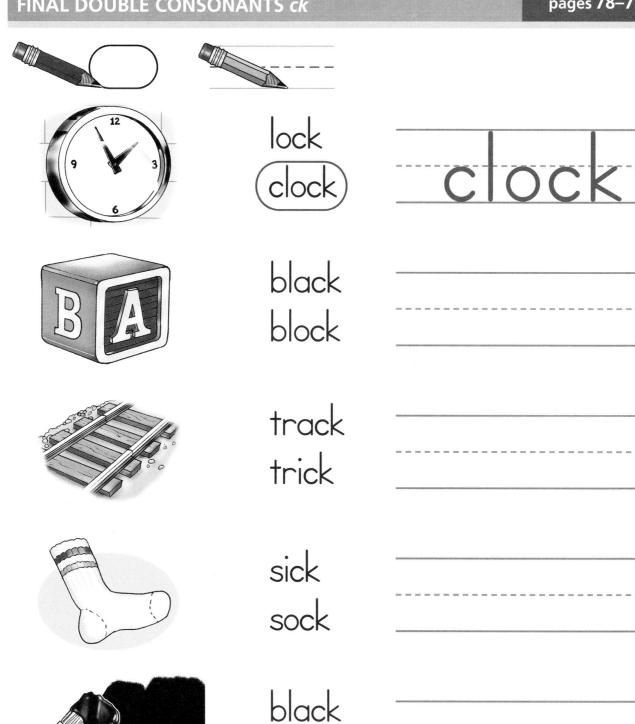

lock
(clock)

clock

black
block

track
trick

sick
sock

black
back

lock   block   sick   stick   back   black

Kick the black rock.   Rick is sick.

| quack | quick | quit | quiz |

 quiz

| quit | kit | quick | kick | crab | quack |

The quill is on the quilt.

133

shop
(shut)

shut

shell
shed

shut
shed

shop
ship

shell
shelf

| shell | sell | hop | shop | hip | ship |

The shell is on the shelf in the shed.

chip
(chop)

chest
check

chin
chick

chimp
chip

chest
chess

chop

ship	chip	shop	chop	chess	chest

The chimp is in the shop. Shut the chest.

th   wh

thick

___in

___en

___ink

___ich

___at

tick	thick	hat	that	hen	when

I think that hat is thick.

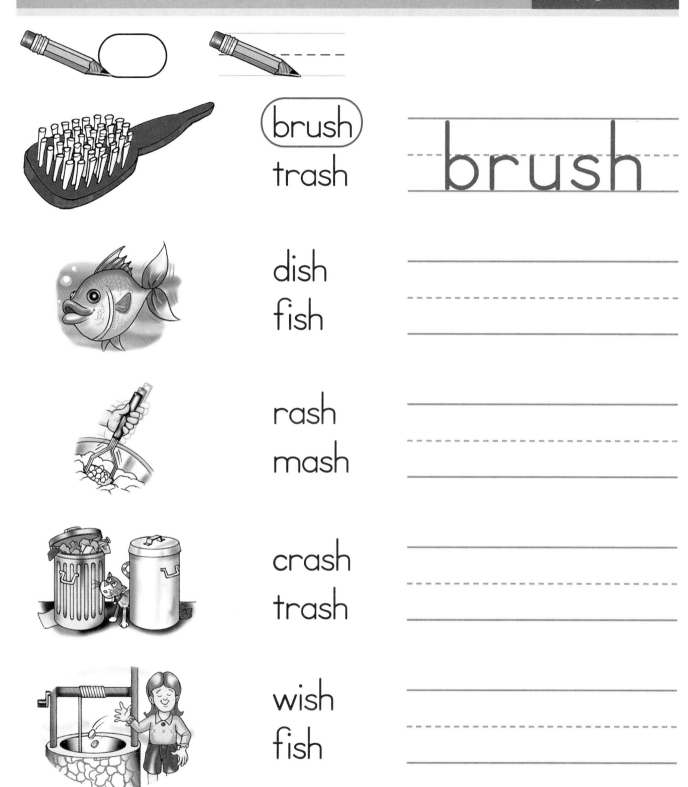

brush
~~trash~~

brush

dish
fish

rash
mash

crash
trash

wish
fish

rash	trash	dish	disk	mash	mask

That brush is in the trash in the shed.

Beth
(Seth)

Seth

with
math

path
bath

bat
bath

with
math

bat   bath   mat   math   Pat   path

Pat is with Seth and Beth on the path.

ang   ing

king

s_____

h_____

sw_____

f_____

sl_____

b_____

s_____

r_____

ran   rang   win   wing   thin   thing

Ring the bell. Ding dong! Ding dong!

139

1. _____   ✔ _____   bring

2. _____   _____

3. _____   _____

4. _____   _____

5. _____   _____

 ab

ank ink unk

p ink

j

b

b

dr

tr

th

w

sk

141

1.  _____   ✔

2.  _____    _____

3.  _____    _____

4.  _____    _____

5.  _____    _____

6.  _____    _____

7.  _____    _____

8.  _____    _____

9.  _____    This is _____

10.  _____    _____

pin	pink	tan	tank	bun	bunk

I think the sink is pink.

(bench)
lunch

 bench

which
rich

inch
pinch

which
lunch

branch
ranch

ran   ranch   pin   pinch   rich   which

Sit on the bench.   Sit on the branch.

143

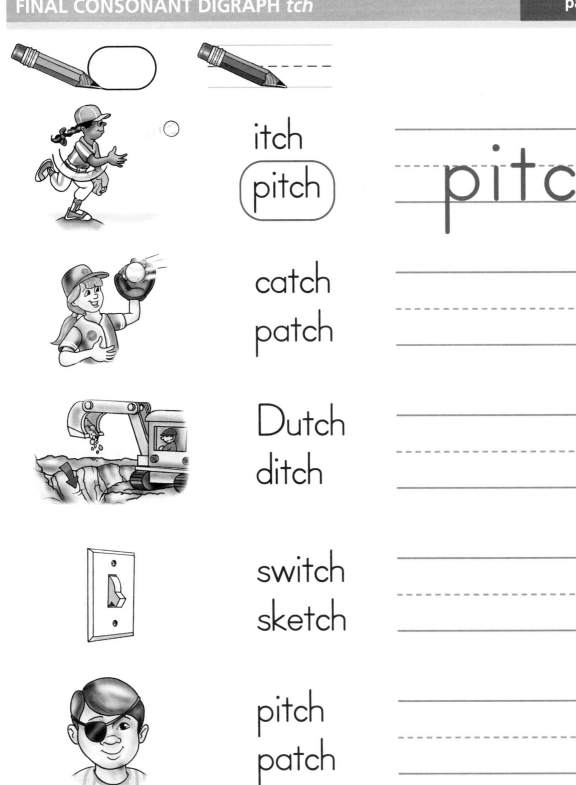

itch
(pitch)

pitch

catch
patch

Dutch
ditch

switch
sketch

pitch
patch

cat   catch   pit   pitch   Pat   patch

Catch the cat in the ditch.

m		(m)	(b)		b
r		r	x		x
ck		ck	ch		ch
s		s	d		d
ch		ch	th		th
sh		sh	th		th

145

   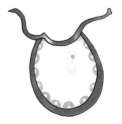

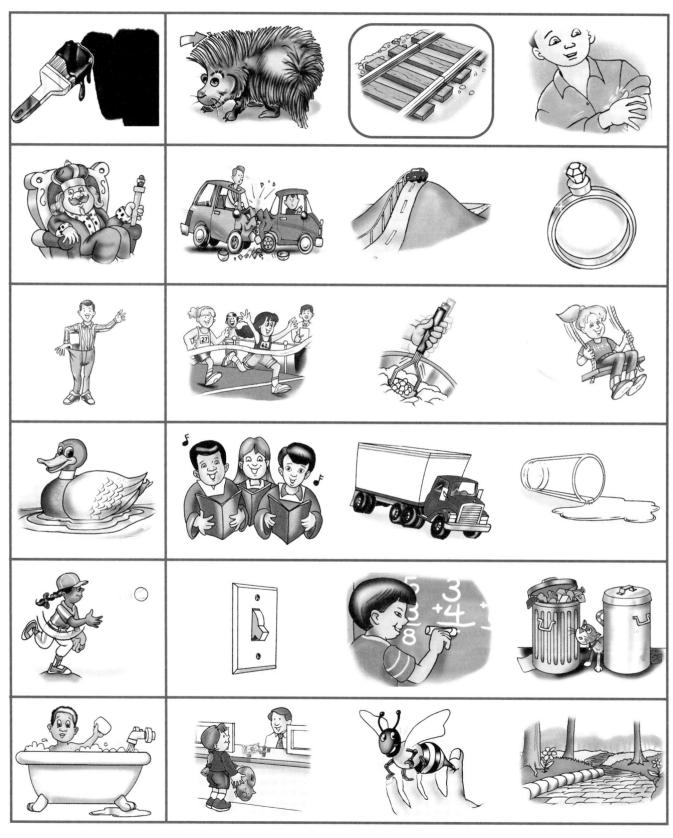

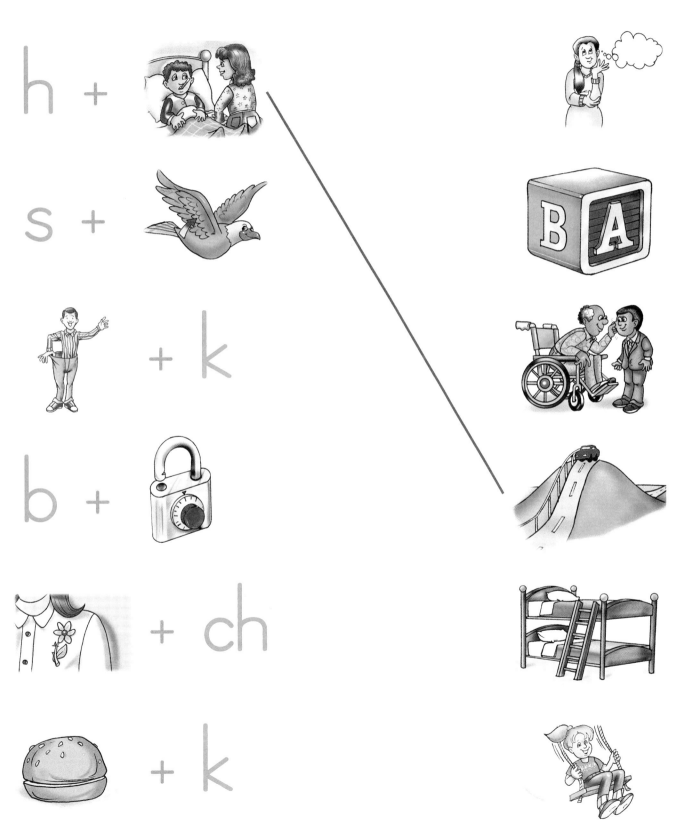

 – d

 – c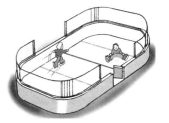

 – s

 – l

 – t

 – ch

chop

 left

 shop

 gift

ship

 lift

stand

 dish

 sang

 disk

 sand

 fish

rake
(cake)

cake

gate
game

mane
name

plate
plane

snake
skate

| can | cane | man | mane | tap | tape |

The rake is at the gate. I ate the cake.

(time)
nine

time

dive
drive

pine
pipe

hike
hide

side
slide

bit   bite   kit   kite   pin   pine

Ride the bike.   Hide on the slide.

note
(home)

home

cone
bone

pole
hole

stove
stole

rode
robe

home   dome   robe   rode   not   note

The mole stole a bone and rode home.

DICTIONARY
pages 116–117

(cube)
tube

cube

dune
duke

prune
flute

dune
tune

rule
rude

cub	cube	cut	cute	tub	tube

Luke is on a mule on a dune in June.

DICTIONARY
pages 110–117

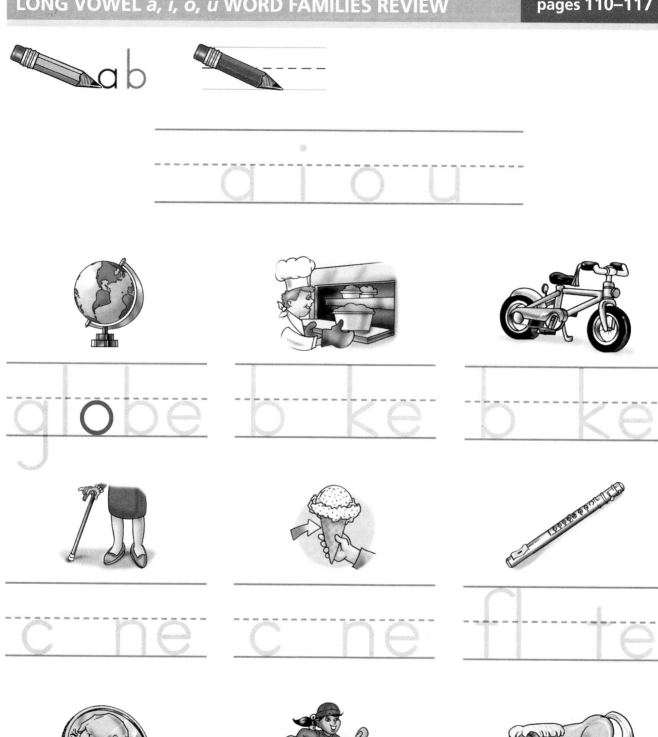

a b

a i o u

globe

b i ke

b i ke

c a ne

c o ne

fl u te

d i me

sk a te

m u le

 + e

_____

 + e

_____

 + e

_____

 + e

cane

 + e

_____

 + e

_____

1. _____   ✔

2. _____   _____

3. _____   _____

4. _____   _____

5. _____   _____

6. _____   _____

7. _____   _____

8. _____   _____

9. _____   _____

10. _____   _____

(bee)
peel

bee

feed
feet

see
seed

three
tree

sweep
sleep

sleep   sweep   sheep   tree   three   green

I see a bee in the green tree.

sea

pea

pea

bead
read

clean
dream

seal
seat

east
eat

| clean | teeth | green | pea | red | bean |

Eat a peach. Clean the seat.

 ab

ee   ea

sheep

l _ _ f

gr _ _ n

b _ _ _

b _ _ n

t _ _ th

sw _ _ p

t _ _ m

qu _ _ n

| go | he | me | no | she | we |

she

| me | meet | she | sheep | no | note |

He and she meet me. We go.

ace ice

race

f_____

m____

st____

br____

r____

ice	rice	race	brace	space	slice

The mice race on the ice.

bunny
(penny)

penny

happy
sleepy

windy
pony

bun
bunny

sleepy
windy

pen penny bun bunny wind windy

The baby is happy. The pony is sleepy.

DICTIONARY
page **127**

	sky	sky
	~~dry~~	
	my / why	
	fry / cry	
	fry / fly	
	dry / fry	

my	pony	sky	windy	cry	baby

Why did my tiny pony cry?

hay
jay

hay

say
day

clay
play

gray
clay

say
jay

| play | plate | May | mane | say | save |

The jay and the snake play a game.

chair
(paint)

paint

rain
train

pail
sail

chain
chair

rain
tail

paint   pail   rain   sail   chain   chair

The gray paint is in the pail on the chair.

ab ____

ay   ai

s**ay**

s__ __

c__

ch__ __n

__t

M____

h____

p____

__nt   pl__

(loaf)
low

loaf

float
blow

toe
toad

hoe
low

crow
grow

| row | road | robe | toad | hoe | home |

Row the boat. Throw the hoe in the hole.

oa   oe   ow

sn**ow**   c _ _ t   _ _ r

  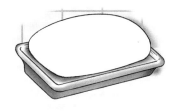

g _ _ t   _ _ t _ _   s _ _ p

h _ _ _   gr _ _   r _ _ d

you
zoo

ZOO

threw
tooth

blew
broom

soup
pool

grew
glue

blue   flew   flute   soup   pool   rule

You threw the new blue tube in the pool.

oo   ou   ew   ue

new   m __ __ n   b l __ __

s p __ __ n   d r __ __   s __ __ p

b __ __ t   __ __ y   f l __ __

| ay | ew | oa | oe | oo | ou | ow | ue |

b**oa**t

b___t

h___

s___p

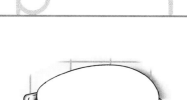

s___p

gr___

gr___

bl___

bl___

fold	roll	bolt	blind	child
hold	toll	colt	find	wild

colt

_____

_____

_____

_____
_____

_____
_____

_____

_____
_____

_____

_____

_____

old	cold	colt	find	kind	child

The roll is cold. The child is kind.

174

car	star	bark	barn	harp
jar	card	park	farm	smart

 barn

car	cart	card	far	farm	arm

The car is in the barn on the farm.

(herd) hurt

herd

corn curl

shirt short

horn herd

skirt shirt

| skirt | shirt | short | fern | turn | corn |

The girl is short.   The bird is hurt.

a b _ _ _

ar er ir or ur

b i r d b _ _ n c _ _ n

g _ _ l t _ _ n n _ _ th

 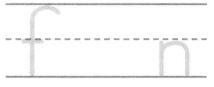 

sh _ _ k f _ _ n sk _ _ t

 + e

 + t

g +

c +

 + e

s +

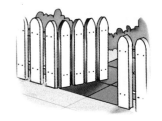

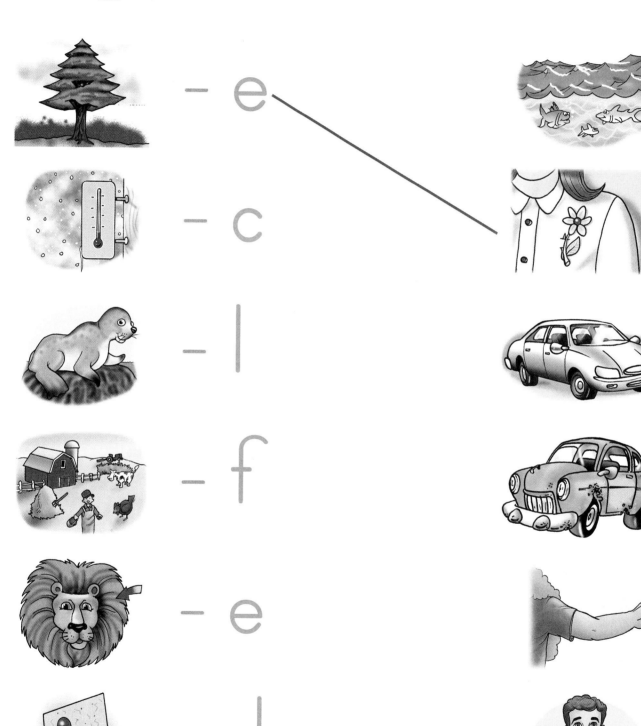

- e

- c

- l

- f

- e

- d

down
(count)

count

bow
how

mouth
mouse

flour
down

owl
our

mouse mouth house how our owl

Our house is round. The owl is brown.

ou   ow

h ou se   c _ _   cl _ _ d

cl _ _ n   m _ se   r _ _ nd

br _ _ n   d _ _ n   sh _ _ t

 a b

oi   oy

coin   b __ __ __ b

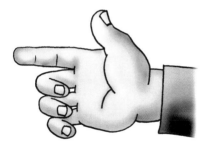

__ __ __ __ l   __ __ t   p __ __ nt

boy   boil   toy   foil   Roy   point

The coin is on the toy.   The oil is in the soil.

  a b

aw au o

 d o g  d r  s ng

 s ce ff s

| saw | say | dog | doll | off | on |

Paul and a dog sang a long song.

| ball | call | fall | small | tall |

The boy is  tall .

I see a big _____ .

The dog is _____ .

When did he _____ ?

We rake in the _____ .

| ball | bag | call | cape | hall | hole |

The wall in the small hall is tall.

door   floor   oar   pour   store

Clean the _floor_ .

She is in the _____ .

The _____ is brown.

Row with the _____ .

I can _____ the milk.

store   stool   pour   pond   roar   road

The oar is on the floor in the store.

| book | full | hook | put | took |

He ___took___ the toy.

Read the _____ .

He is _____ .

The cap is on the _____ .

She _____ it on the shelf.

| book | moon | pull | rule | bull | mule |

Push and pull the door. Look at the bull.

sleigh
light

light

weight
high

bright
brought

caught
taught

eighty
eight

eight   weight   weigh   high   thought   taught

She caught the ball and brought it home.

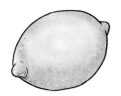    

| 1 | ② | ① | 2 | 1 | 2 | 1 | 2 |

| 1 | 2 | 1 | 2 | 1 | 2 | 1 | 2 |

| 1 | 2 | 1 | 2 | 1 | 2 | 1 | 2 |

| 1 | 2 | 1 | 2 | 1 | 2 | 1 | 2 |

| 1 | 2 | 1 | 2 | 1 | 2 | 1 | 2 |

189

| b | d | k | g | m | n | p | v | w |

ca b in   wa on   pa er

ba er   pla et   flo er

 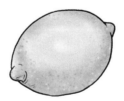 

Fri ay   le on   o er

cabin wagon paper baker flower broken

The spider is on the flower in the cabin.

| bb | dd | ll | mm | nn | pp | tt |

di**nn**er   le___er   ra___it

bu___er   zi___er   la___er

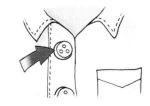

ha___er   ye___ow   bu___on

lad   ladder   zip   zipper   pup   puppet

Follow the kitten. The mitten is yellow.

| kitten | mitten | muffin | pillow | puppet | summer |

The **kitten** is cute.

We swim in the _____ .

I ate a _____ .

The _____ is on the bed.

The _____ is on my hand.

The _____ is blue.

ck ft nc nd nt rt st

dirty   wi___ow   fi___een

chi___en   pe___il   ___u___er

wi___er   ja___et   si___er

pen   pencil   sun   Sunday   win   window

The jacket is dirty. The pencil is on the blanket.

| angry | blanket | doctor | father | finger | pencil |

He is my __father__.

This is my _____.

She is _____.

I went to the _____.

I hurt my _____.

The _____ is blue.

above
glove

glove

money
honey

brother
mother

bread
thread

feather
weather

mother   mom   honey   home   head   hat

The sweater on the monkey is heavy.

(table)
steeple

table

poodle
noodle

beetle
turtle

bubble
purple

little
middle

needle noodle puddle poodle little middle

The turtle and the purple beetle did a puzzle.

| apple | circle | cradle | eagle | needle | puddle |

The **eagle** can fly.

The _____ is red.

The _____ is round.

The _____ is sharp.

She is in the _____.

The baby is in the _____.

197

DICTIONARY
pages 166–167

b   h   k   l   t   w

w rist   ta k   nee

w ite   am   lis en

rong   ca f   w ale

Climb	Knit	Knock	Wrap	Write

Knit a sweater.

_____ the gift.

_____ up high.

_____ a letter.

_____ on the door.

kit	knit	white	write	hall	half

The lamb and the calf walk and talk.

199

s   es

pen**s**   book   box

bike   globe   watch

seat   pencil   glass

maps   books   pens   rulers   brushes   watches

The books and the pencils are in the boxes.

leaf

loaf

fly

penny

wolf

shelf

leaves

fly   flies   leaf   leaves   half   halves

The babies play with the calves and the puppies.

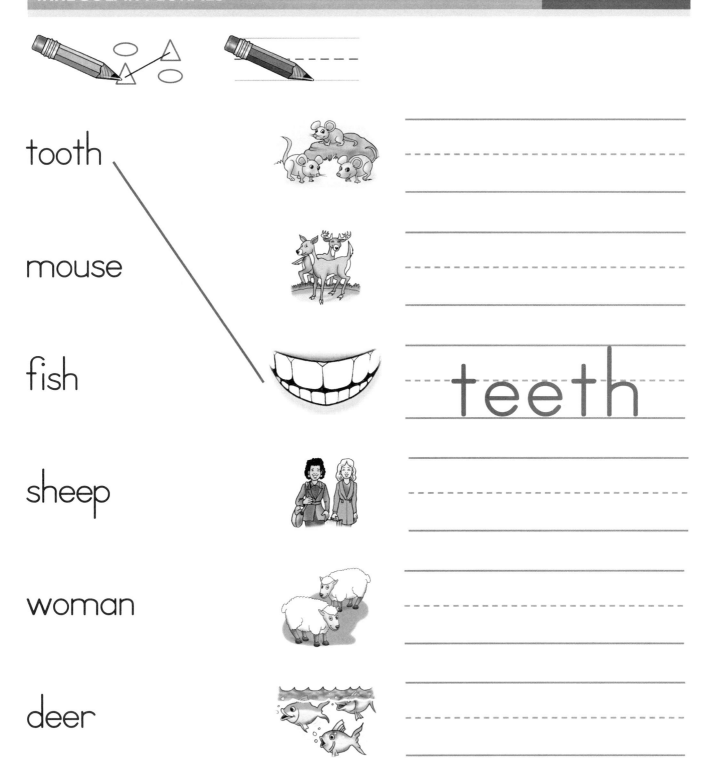

tooth

mouse

fish

teeth

sheep

woman

deer

| foot | feet | mouse | mice | man | men |

The children see the geese, mice, and sheep.

1. _____   ✔_____   2.
  _____

3.
  _____   _____   4.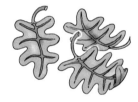
  _____

5.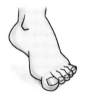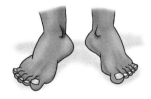
  _____   _____   6.
  _____

7.
  _____   _____   8.
  _____

9. _____   _____   10. _____   _____

| scr | spl | spr | str | squ |

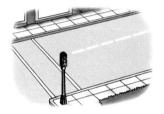  

str**eet** ___ash ___ay

___ing ___ing ___are

___eam ___aw ___atch

| ring | string | spring | lit | split | splash |

Splash in the spring. Stretch the string.

s	es

I cook and he ___cooks___ .

I add and she _____ .

We work and she _____ .

I clean and he _____ .

You play and she _____ .

I brush and he _____ .

talk	talks	pull	pulls	push	pushes

I cook, he cleans, and she works.

ed

I brushed my teeth.

Mom _____ .

Dad _____ .

He _____ the floor.

She _____ on the slide.

She _____ with the chalk.

walk   walked   listen   listened   point   pointed

You talked.   I listened.   He shouted.

206

| cooking | drawing | painting | playing | singing | throwing |

I'm ___cooking___ lunch.

She's _____ a ball.

He's _____ the wall.

We're _____ in the yard.

You're _____ a flower.

They're _____ a song.

| cried | dropped | riding | running | sitting | writing |

He's ___sitting___ at a desk.

We're _____ fast.

I'm _____ a letter.

The little boy _____.

She's _____ a bike.

You _____ the ball.

A _teacher_ can teach.

A _____ can sing.

A _____ can bake.

A _____ can swim.

A _____ can paint.

An _____ can act.

farmer conductor shopper jogger winner

My teacher is a good singer and dancer.

busy	cheese	hose	these	has
easy	choose	rose	those	

rose

_____

_____

those   bees   has   flies   peas   is

Please close the door. My nose smells a rose.

g	gh	ph

ph_one _____iant _____oto

lar__e lau__ dol__in

cou__ __iraffe gra__

phone	alphabet	graph	laugh	giant	orange

The dolphin and the elephant laugh at the giraffe.

come	have	said	was
give	none	some	were

was

Come home. Give me a dime.

I have some and he has none.

The painter said some paint was in the pail.

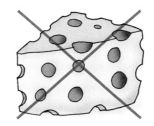

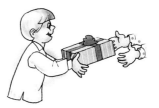

213

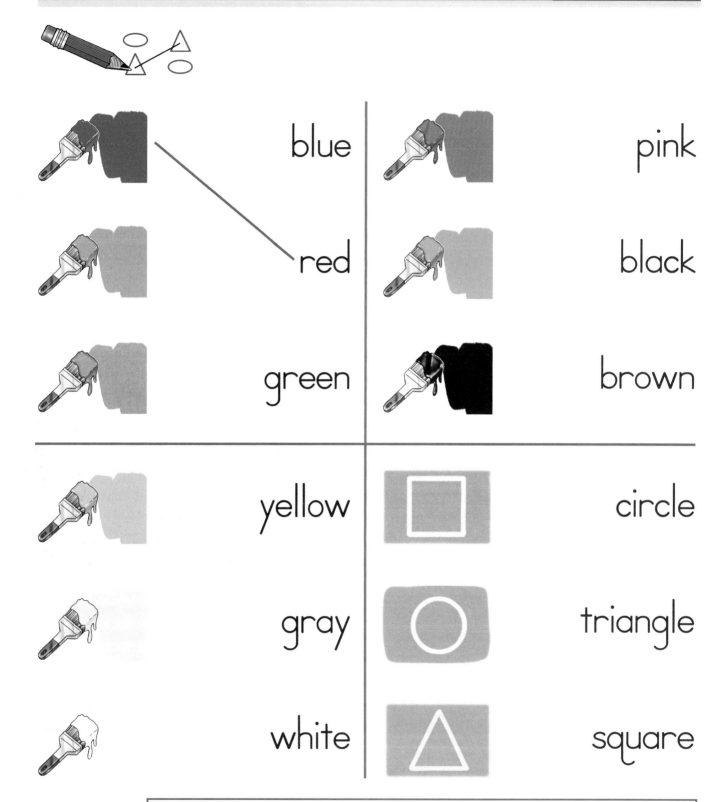

blue

red

green

yellow

gray

white

pink

black

brown

circle

triangle

square

That cow is brown, black, and white.

My shirt is blue, red, and green.

 **? ?**

| black | circle | green | oval | pink | rectangle | red | square |

Colors

black

Shapes

circle

book

pencil

hat

skirt

doll

globe

cap

crayon

desk

chair

shirt

yo-yo

Put the book and the pencil on the desk.

The doll has a skirt, a sweater, and sneakers.

? ?

| book | cap | coat | desk | doll | dress | hat | yo-yo |

Objects & Toys

Clothing

book

cap

217

nut

pea

egg

rice

lemon

corn

ham

milk

apple

meat

cheese

cake

We're eating meat, rice, beans, and bread.

I'm baking muffins with butter and honey.

? ?

| boot | cake | cap | coat | fig | ham | hat | pea |

Clothing

Food

boot

goat

sheep

skunk

camel

flower

eagle

crow

cow

owl

boy

jay

bee

The bee is on the flower with the ant.

The girl and boy see a rabbit in a bush.

| crow | eagle | fox | jay | monkey | owl | rabbit | skunk |

Animals

Birds

crow

er   est

tall

This bag is heavy. That bag is heavier.

The train is faster than the car.

The biggest plane is the fastest.

ship

sad

large

bunny

unhappy

rabbit

big

boat

small

present

song

store

shop

little

tune

gift

| Shut the door. Close the window. |
| Sing a song. Play a tune. |

day
night

new
old

push
pull

over
under

right
left

last
first

night

Push it. Pull it. Open it. Close it.

The day was hot and the night was cold.

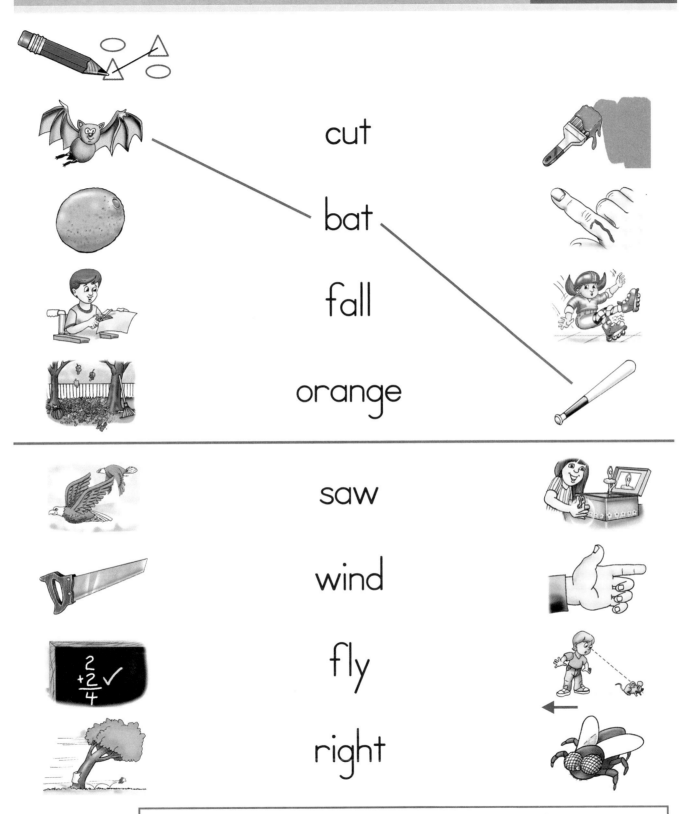

cut

bat

fall

orange

saw

wind

fly

right

An orange is orange. Wind the top.

Leaves fall with the wind in the fall.

 right
(write)

  ate
eight

 meet
meat

 see
sea

 flour
flower

 meet
meat

 eight
ate

 right
write

 wrap
rap

 flour
flower

 sea
see

 wrap
rap

We meet and rap. Wrap the meat.

I see eight flowers in the sea.

| dis | re | un | ful | less | ly |

quickly

turn

fold

home

connect

slow

care

write

Rewrite the letter slowly.

See the playful rabbit disappear quickly.

 +  =  rainbow

 +  =

 + =

 + =

 + =

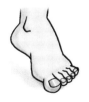 + =

 + =

The notebook is on the bookshelf in the classroom.

The football is in the sandbox in the backyard.

228

1 2 3 4 5

   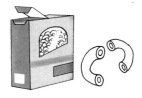

3 ___   ___   ___   ___

  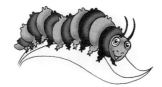 

___   ___   ___   ___

___   ___   ___   ___

___   ___   ___   ___

A grasshopper and a dragonfly met a caterpillar.

The alligator and the hippopotamus talked with the kangaroo and the porcupine.

229

big

(little)

cheese

choose

chair

desk

spring

string

shop

boat

soap

soup

print

paint

tub

tube

write

right

shirt

skirt

right

left

sea

see

penny

pennies

mouse

mice

1.

 ✔

box

2.

3.

4.

5.

6. _____ _____

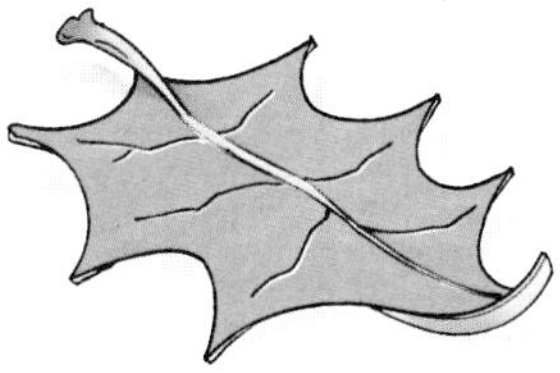

7. _____ _____

8. _____ _____

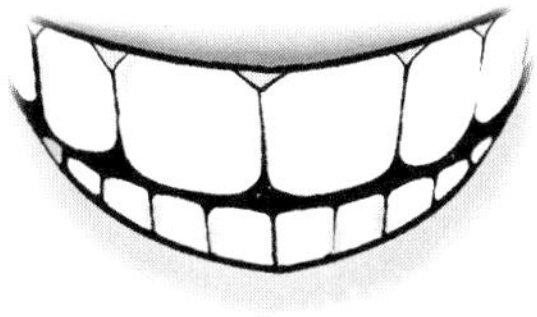

9. _____ _____

10. _____ _____

11. _____ _____

PAGE 27
Listen and choose the correct picture.
1. pit
2. zip
3. bat
4. cap
5. pig

PAGE 50
Listen and choose the correct picture.
1. pin
2. get
3. jug
4. hen
5. fog

PAGE 51
Listen and choose the correct picture.
1. pig
2. can
3. map
4. bug
5. hot

PAGE 62
Listen and choose the correct picture.
1. bag
2. tag
3. wag
4. ham
5. dam

PAGE 85
Listen and choose the correct picture.
1. ill
2. egg
3. add
4. up
5. on

PAGE 88
Listen and choose the correct picture.
1. mud
2. mom
3. nut
4. net
5. man

PAGE 91
Listen and choose the correct picture.
1. set
2. fan
3. sit
4. fog
5. sun

PAGE 94
Listen and choose the correct picture.
1. hit
2. hog
3. job
4. jug
5. ham

PAGE 97
Listen and choose the correct picture.
1. log
2. run
3. lip
4. lap
5. red

PAGE 100
Listen and choose the correct picture.
1. pet
2. bat
3. pin
4. pup
5. big

PAGE 103
Listen and choose the correct picture.
1. tag
2. dig
3. top
4. ten
5. dip

PAGE 106
Listen and choose the correct picture.
1. get
2. cub
3. cat
4. gum
5. got

PAGE 120
Listen and choose the correct picture.
1. ran
2. spin
3. lap
4. spot
5. slip
6. top
7. flip
8. clap
9. frog
10. flat

PAGE 127
Listen and choose the correct picture.
1. wind
2. wet
3. fist
4. band
5. net
6. went
7. sad
8. vest
9. list
10. lift

PAGE 140
Listen and choose the correct picture.
1. bring
2. wing
3. sting
4. thing
5. rang

PAGE 142
Listen and choose the correct picture.
1. rink
2. sing
3. wing
4. think
5. bank
6. thank
7. sting
8. drink
9. blank
10. stink

PAGE 158
Listen and choose the correct picture.
1. cape
2. tube
3. cut
4. pine
5. tap
6. mane
7. kite
8. can
9. note
10. cube

PAGE 203
Listen and choose the correct picture.
1. bikes
2. glass
3. puppies
4. mice
5. tooth
6. leaf
7. feet
8. book
9. pens
10. men

PAGES 232–233
Listen and choose the correct picture.
1. box
2. stop
3. sink
4. name
5. fog
6. skate
7. leaf
8. winter
9. teeth
10. turtle
11. cleaned

(A complete Answer Key for this workbook may be found in the *Word by Word Primary* Teacher's Guide.)

	📖	Read (silently and aloud). Practice individually, with a partner, and as a class.
	✏️ a b	Trace.
	✏️ - - - -	Write.
	✏️ ◯ or ✏️ ⬭	Choose the correct answer. (Put a circle or oval around it.)
	✏️ ⬭ ✏️ - - - -	Choose the correct answer. Then write the word.
	🎧 ✏️ ◯	Listen and choose the correct answer.
	🎧 ✏️ ✓	Listen and put a check under the correct picture.
	🎧 ✏️ ✓ ✏️ - - - -	Listen and put a check under the correct picture. Later, write a word for each picture you checked.
	✏️ ✗	Put an X on the picture that doesn't belong with the others.
	✏️ ◯ △ △ ◯	Draw a line to match the item on the left with the correct item on the right.
	✏️ ? ?	Write each word from the box under the correct category.

Give children the opportunity to hear and say all words in all activities throughout this workbook. Children can do the activities silently in school or at home and then practice saying the words aloud as a class, with another child, or with a tutor, aide, parent, or other adult.